Have You Ever Met a Yeti?

Have you ever seen a yeti? Or a unicorn? Maybe, just maybe, these magical creatures could be real …

This picture book targets the /y/ sound and is part of *Speech Bubbles 2*, a series of picture books that target specific speech sounds within the story.

The series can be used for children receiving speech therapy, for children who have a speech sound delay/disorder, or simply as an activity for children's speech sound development and/or phonological awareness. They are ideal for use by parents, teachers or caregivers.

Bright pictures and a fun story create an engaging activity perfect for sound awareness.

Picture books are sold individually, or in a pack. There are currently two packs available – *Speech Bubbles 1* and *Speech Bubbles 2*. Please see further titles in the series for stories targeting other speech sounds.

Melissa Palmer is a Speech Language Therapist. She worked for the Ministry of Education, Special Education in New Zealand from 2008 to 2013, with children aged primarily between 2 and 8 years of age. She also completed a diploma in children's writing in 2009, studying under author Janice Marriott, through the New Zealand Business Institute. Melissa has a passion for articulation and phonology, as well as writing and art, and has combined these two loves to create *Speech Bubbles*.

T0056255

What's in the pack?

User Guide

Vinnie the Dove

Rick's Carrot

Harry the Hopper

Have You Ever Met a Yeti?

Zack the Buzzy Bee

Asher the Thresher Shark

Catch That Chicken!

Will the Wolf

Magic Licking Lollipops

Jasper the Badger

Platypus and Fly

The Dragon Drawing War

Have You Ever Met a Yeti?

Targeting the /y/ Sound

Melissa Palmer

Routledge
Taylor & Francis Group

LONDON AND NEW YORK

First published 2021
by Routledge
2 Park Square, Milton Park, Abingdon, Oxon OX14 4RN

and by Routledge
52 Vanderbilt Avenue, New York, NY 10017

Routledge is an imprint of the Taylor & Francis Group, an informa business

British Library Cataloguing-in-Publication Data
A catalogue record for this book is available from the British Library

Library of Congress Cataloging-in-Publication Data
Names: Palmer, Melissa (Speech language therapist) author.
Title: Have you ever met a Yeti? : targeting the y sound / Melissa Palmer.
Description: Milton Park, Abingdon, Oxon ; New York, NY : Routledge, 2021. |
Series: Speech bubbles 2 Identifiers: LCCN 2020048822 (print) | LCCN 2020048823 (ebook) |
ISBN 9780367648589 (paperback) | ISBN 9781003126614 (ebook)
Subjects: LCSH: Speech therapy for children–Juvenile literature. |
Speech therapy–Juvenile literature. | Articulation disorders in children–Juvenile
literature. | Yeti–Juvenile literature.
Classification: LCC RJ496.S7 P32 2021 (print) | LCC RJ496.S7 (ebook) |
DDC 618.92/85506–dc23 LC record available at https://lccn.loc.gov/2020048822
LC ebook record available at https://lccn.loc.gov/2020048823

ISBN: 978-1-138-59784-6 (set)
ISBN: 978-0-367-64858-9 (pbk)
ISBN: 978-1-003-12661-4 (ebk)

Typeset in Calibri
by Newgen Publishing UK

Have You Ever Met a Yeti?

Have **y**ou ever seen a **y**eti

Eat a bowl of spaghetti?

With **y**ellow teeth and a gi**a**nt jaw,

Carr**y**ing a bunch of on**io**ns in its paw?

I met a **y**eti called Br**ia**n – I swear I'm not l**y**ing!

He had **y**ellow teeth and a g**ia**nt head,

He had a mound of **y**oung **y**ams for his bed.

His hair was fuzz**ie**st round his tummy,

He thought **y**ellow **y**olk was particularly **y**ummy.

Br**ia**n loved to sit and **y**ell at the moon,

On top of his **y**urt where he will fall asleep soon.

You might think he's the scar**ie**st with all his brawn,

Until he rubs his eyes with a **y**awn.

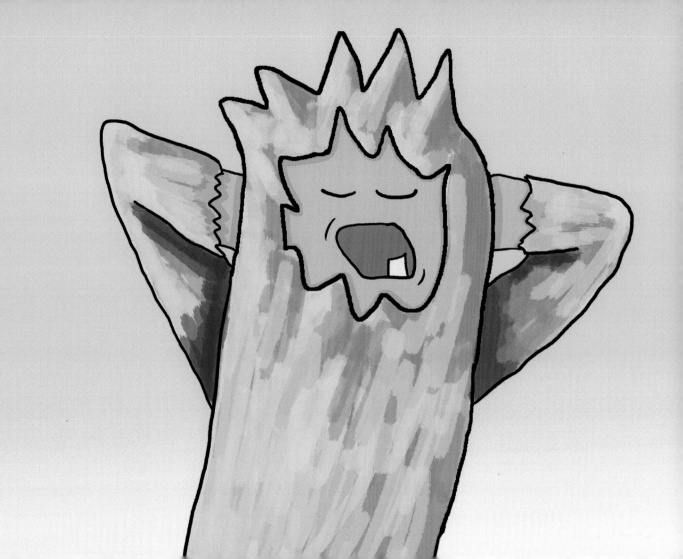

His best friend is **Y**arny **Y**ak,

With **y**ellow hair down his back.

-y-y-y-y-y-y-y-y-y-y-y Yarny's laugh was quite strange.

Yeti's jokes are the funn**ie**st and that won't change.

You don't believe me? That **y**etis are real?

You could be right, I feel …

I wonder…

Perhaps it was a dream – I've had it all **y**ear.

Maybe Br**ia**n isn't real at all, I fear!

But I must tell **y**ou – please don't scorn –

I know for SURE I've met a **u**nicorn!